PREDATOR AND PREY

A CONVERSATION IN VERSE

PREDATOR AND PREY

A CONVERSATION IN VERSE

Susannah Buhrman-Deever

illustrated by Bert Kitchen

CANDLEWICK STUDIO

an imprint of Candlewick Press

Predators and prey are locked in a battle for survival.

Predators need food to live.

        Prey don't want to be eaten.

We often think of predators and prey doing battle with weapons like claws and teeth or using speed and strength. But they also use other tricks.

Prey use their voices for defense.

Predators and prey can both be spies, listening in on each other's conversations.

They even talk to each other.

        Sometimes they tell the truth.

            Sometimes they lie.

Whatever methods they use, both predators and prey have the same goal: to survive and raise young.

And they both fight to win.

Spies (A Poem for Two Voices)

Toon-chuck-chuck!
We form a throng
Toon-chuck-chuck!
In soggy ponds

Toon-chuck-chuck!
Our throats inflate
Toon-chuck-chuck!
We call for mates

Toon-chuck-chuck!
Our chuck notes boom
Toon-chuck-chuck!
And females swoon

Toon-chuck-chuck!

We hear you too
Toon-chuck-chuck!

You foolish crew
Toon-chuck-chuck!

We listen in
Toon-chuck-chuck!

To froggy din
Toon-chuck-chuck!

With every chuck

What Webs We Weave (A Poem for Two Voices)

I am hunter	I am hunter
I weave the web	
I lie in wait	
	I pluck the threads
	I play the bait
I listen for	
	My siren song?
the tremors of wings	the tremors of wings
caught on strings	caught on strings
I am	
insect catcher	
	I am
	puppet master,
	spider snatcher
	I am hunter

Assassin Bug and Spider

Though assassin bugs look delicate, they are well named. Assassin bugs stab their prey with strong, straw-like "beaks," injecting it with digestive juices that dissolve the prey from the inside out.

One species of assassin bug from Australia hunts spiders. Spiders "listen" to the movements of their webs to learn when prey has been caught. The assassin bug takes advantage of this. The bug plucks the silken threads of the spider's web with its front legs to mimic the movements a trapped insect would make. The spider goes in for the kill, but the assassin bug is the one to get the meal.

Unlucky in Love

I am hungry
for love.
Flashing,
I seek you.
A light in the dark!
My treasure!

Femme Fatale

My treasure?
A light in the dark.
I seek you,
flashing
for love.
I am hungry.

Female Pennsylvania Fireflies and Male Big Dipper Fireflies

The magical flashes of fireflies on summer nights are really a lively dating scene. Male fireflies flash to get a female's attention. Females flash back so the males can find them. Each species of firefly has its own code—a flashing call-and-response rhythm that helps males and females of the same species find each other.

Female Pennsylvania fireflies can lie. They flash back to male big dipper fireflies using the big dipper code. The tricked males fly down, thinking they have found a mate. Instead, they become dinner. Why play such a deadly trick? Big dipper males have poisonous chemicals in their bodies that protect them from predators. By eating the males, Pennsylvania firefly females can get those chemicals for themselves.

Ant Armies

We are a force of fearsome troops
We scout the stems for prey
We leave a scent trail to recruit
More fighters for the fray
Even stingers are no match
For our army's blitz attack
Our pincers bite; we pull, we burn
The bees will fall before our swarm

The Scent of Danger

Flower nectar, a scent so sweet
Detected from the air
But a spicy note of danger says
I'll quench my thirst elsewhere

Weaver Ant and Giant Honey Bee

Weaver ants search plants for their insect prey. The ants lay a scent trail as they walk. Other ants follow the trail to help them stay together. Like a wolf pack, many ants work together to attack.

If given the chance, weaver ants will kill honey bees visiting a plant's flowers. But giant honey bees can detect the ants' scent trail, and they avoid flowers that smell like an ant patrol. The honey bees are paying attention to their predators to avoid being eaten.

A Call to Arms

Alarm! Alarm! Alarm!
Friends and flock mates, comrades all!
Come and heed my battle call!
Let's peck and pester, twitter-bomb!
With whirls of wings our feisty mob
will drive this hunter from our trees—
the hawk will flee from chickadees!
Attack! Attack! Attack!

Sharp-Shinned Hawk and Chickadee

A sharp-shinned hawk is designed for surprise aerial attacks. A perched sharp-shinned hawk isn't an immediate threat, but chickadees don't want it around. They use loud, repeated mobbing calls to gather the flock together and drive the predator away.

A hawk on the wing is a greater danger. If a chickadee spots a flying hawk, it makes a seet alarm call—a soft, high-pitched whistle. It's very hard for a hawk to tell where this type of sound is coming from, so the calling chickadee stays hidden. But other birds nearby hear the message: lie low; danger is near.

PSST-HIDE!

seet

      (*Psst*-Hide!)

           (I warn of airborne storms

           but save myself

           with vocal stealth.)

The Sharp-Shinned Hawk's Reply

Today
you may have won
but there will be a time
when the first
hint
of me
will be
the feel
of my talons
as they strike
your fluttering
heart

Patience of a Snake

I am patient.
I am primed.
I am coiled muscle,
expertly designed.
I am loaded spring
I am . . .
          LIGHTNING!

Hot-Tempered Squirrel

I'm hot
and bothered.
I'm hot
under the collar.
I'm fur-rious
F U R I O U S !
Flag waving,
I boldly scold:
"Hey, you! Get off my lawn!!"

Pacific Rattlesnake and Ground Squirrel

Rattlesnakes wait, hidden and ready, until an unsuspecting animal gets close. Rattlesnakes attack ground squirrels, but ground squirrels do not always seem to be afraid of them. They often walk right up to a waiting rattlesnake, heating up and boldly waving their tails.

Why? The squirrels are telling the snake, "I know you're there!" Rattlesnakes can sense heat. A hot tail makes the squirrel's tail-waving "I see you" message louder. After an adult squirrel taunts a snake, the snake is less likely to strike, and more likely to leave. It knows it has lost the element of surprise.

Sound Wars

(A Poem for Two Voices)

Chirp!

 Beware

Chirp!

 the air

I scan the skies

To find my prize

Chirp!

 I hound

Chirp!

 with sound

My keen sound-sight

Makes darkness bright

Chirp!

 My sound

Chirp!

 Rebounds

The echoes sing

Off small moth wings

Chirp! Chirp! Chirp!

The echoes fast

Chirp! Chirp! Chirp!

This moth won't last

Chirp! Chirp! Chirp!

It's close, it's near

Chirp! Chir—

 CLICK!CLICK!CLICK!CLICK!CLICK!CLICK!

Wait—did it just disappear?

Big Brown Bat and Tiger Moth

Big brown bats use echolocation to find their prey in the dark. They make high-pitched sounds as they hunt. The sounds bounce off objects in the environment, creating echoes that help them find their prey.

A tiger moth can jam the bat's echolocation. Just as the bat makes its final approach, the tiger moth makes loud, fast clicks. The clicks interfere with the echo pattern of the bat's sounds, and the bat loses track of the moth, giving the moth enough time to dodge out of harm's way.

Don't Eat Here

Bright colors, bold stripes
Warning flags, stoplights
Neon signs to advertise
Dining here would not be wise

Blue Jay, Monarch Butterfly, and Zebra Longwing Butterfly

Many animals are protected with poisons. They also display bright colors and patterns to let predators know that they are not good to eat. Predators learn that bright colors mean bad taste, so they don't attack. This keeps the brightly colored animal from being eaten, and the predator is saved from a mouthful of poison—a win-win.

Look-Alikes

Admiral   and   Swallowtail
red-spotted, dusky pale
blue wings with black veins
almost twins,
almost the same.
                        One is honest;
one's a cheat.
                        One is poison;
one is sweet.
                How do I choose
                which one to eat?

Blue Jay, Pipevine Swallowtail Butterfly, and Red-Spotted Purple Admiral Butterfly

Some animals take advantage of another's bad taste. The tasty red-spotted purple admiral butterfly looks very similar to the highly poisonous pipevine swallowtail. Insect-eating birds avoid them both, so the cheater admirals get away for free.

Startling Beauty

In winter twilight

or summer sun

In frosty slumber

or nectar drunk

I rest,
cloaked in quiet,
a silent prayer

until
you come
curious and hungry

snuffling, whiskering

twittering, pecking

then
I spread
my uproarious, glorious wings
and you
take flight

What Is That? (A Poem for Two Voices)

	I flit
I scurry	
	I hop
I sneak	
tasty bugs	tasty bugs
and grubs	and grubs
I seek	I seek
That hiss!	
	Those eyes!
Flee!	Flee!
Eek!	Eek!

Peacock Butterfly, Blue Tit, and Yellow-Necked Mouse

A peacock butterfly hides by blending in. It rests with its wings closed, looking dull and brown, like a piece of bark or a dead leaf. But if a predator gets too close, it has another trick. The butterfly snaps its wings open. The opening wings make a hissing sound and show off bright blue and yellow eye-shaped spots. This startling display scares off insect-eating birds.

Peacock butterflies hibernate through the winter in dark places—in cracks between rocks, tree hollows, and unheated buildings. But they still use the wing display in the dark. The sudden hissing sound scares off curious and hungry mice.

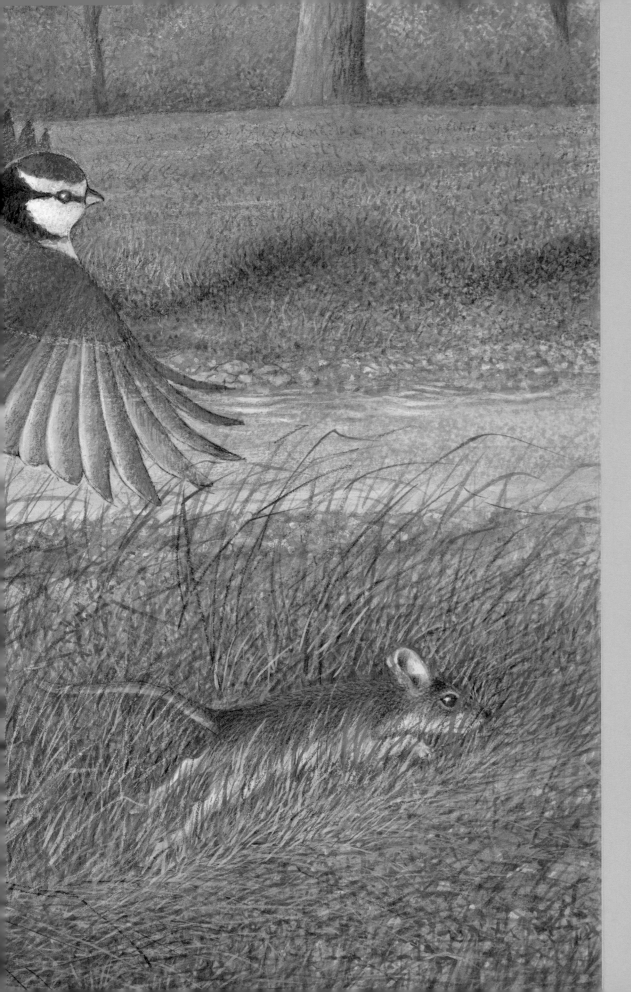

Shadow Striker

Stealthy
shadow hunter,
sprinter, stunner, am I.
You, Lizard? Target of my dark
embrace.

Push-up Power

I'm buff!
I'm tough!
You know I've got the stuff!

My push-up moves
Will prove to you
My legs are strong
I've got the brawn
    (You sure you wanna
     take me on?)

'Cuz I'm buff!
And I'm tough!
And you know I've got the stuff!

Puerto Rican Racer and Crested Anole Lizard

Anole lizards are one of the favorite foods of the Puerto Rican racer. But if an anole spots a racer approaching, it might start doing push-ups instead of running away. Why the push-up display? When a racer catches an anole, the anole usually puts up a fight. It may wrestle and bite the snake for up to half an hour. The snake could get injured and might not get a meal. Anoles do push-ups to show off their strength. Racers are less likely to attack an anole who can do a lot of push-ups. It's just not worth the trouble.

Bibliography

Abt, K. F., and Walter F. Bock. "Seasonal Variations of Diet Composition in Farmland Field Mice *Apodemus* spp. and Bank Voles *Clethrionomys glareolus*." *Acta Theriologica* 43, no. 4 (1998): 379–389.

All About Birds (Cornell Lab of Ornithology). "Sharp-shinned Hawk." Accessed April 2, 2013. http://www.allaboutbirds.org/guide/Sharp-shinned_Hawk/id.

Arkive. "Yellow-Necked Mouse (*Apodemus flavicollis*)." Accessed February 15, 2015. http://www.arkive.org/yellow-necked-mouse/apodemus-flavicollis.

Barbour, Matthew A., and Rulon W. Clark. 2012. "Ground Squirrel Tail-Flag Displays Alter Both Predatory Strike and Ambush Site Selection Behaviours of Rattlesnakes." *Proceedings of the Royal Society B: Biological Sciences*. http://rspb.royalsocietypublishing.org/content/279/1743/3827.

Blue Tit Blog. British Trust for Ornithology. Accessed March 14, 2015. http://www.bto.org/volunteer-surveys/nbc/blue-tit-blog.

Bradbury, Jack W., and Sandra L. Vehrencamp. *Principles of Animal Communication*, 2nd ed. Sunderland, MA: Sinauer, 2011.

Catchpole, C. K., and P. J. B. Slater. *Bird Song: Biological Themes and Variations*. Cambridge: Cambridge University Press, 1995.

Corcoran, Aaron J., Jesse R. Barber, and William E. Conner. "Tiger Moth Jams Bat Sonar." *Science* 325, no. 5936 (2009): 325–327.

De Bona, Sebastiano, Janne K. Valkonen, Andrés Lopez-Sepulcre, and Johanna Mappes. "Predator Mimicry, Not Conspicuousness, Explains the Efficacy of Butterfly Eyespots." *Proceedings of the Royal Society B: Biological Sciences* 282 (2015): 20150202.

Eisner, Thomas, Michael A. Goetz, David E. Hill, Scott R. Smedley, and Jerrold Meinwald. "Firefly 'Femmes Fatales' Acquire Defensive Steroids (Lucibufagins) from Their Firefly Prey." *Proceedings of the National Academy of Sciences* 94 (1997): 9723–9728.

Halfwerk, W., P. L. Jones, R. C. Taylor, M. J. Ryan, and R. A. Page. "Risky Ripples Allow Bats and Frogs to Eavesdrop on a Multisensory Sexual Display." *Science* 343, no. 6169 (2014): 413–416. DOI: 10.1126/science.1244812.

Leal, Manuel. "Honest Signalling During Prey-Predator Interactions in the Lizard *Anolis cristatellus*." *Animal Behaviour* 58 (1999): 521–526.

Leal, Manuel, and Javier A. Rodríguez-Robles. "Antipredator Responses of *Anolis cristatellus* (Sauria: Polychrotidae)." *Copeia* 1995, no. 1 (1995): 155–161.

———. "Signalling Displays During Predator-Prey Interactions in a Puerto Rican Anole, *Anolis cristatellus*." *Animal Behaviour* 54 (1997): 1147–1154.

Li, Jianjun, Zhengwei Wang, Ken Tan, Yufeng Qu, and James C. Nieh. "Giant Asian Honeybees Use Olfactory Eavesdropping to Detect and Avoid Ant Predators." *Animal Behaviour* 97 (2014): 69–76.

Lloyd, James E. "Aggressive Mimicry in Photuris: Firefly Femmes Fatales." *Science* 149, no. 3684 (1965): 653–654.

The Mammal Society website. "Yellow-Necked Mouse (*Apodemus flavicollis*)." Accessed January 10, 2015. http://www.mammal.org.uk/species-factsheets/Yellow-necked%20 mouse.

National Wildlife Federation. "Fireflies." Accessed May 10, 2016. https://www.nwf.org/ Wildlife/Wildlife-Library/Invertebrates/Firefly.aspx.

Olofsson, Martin, Adrian Vallin, Sven Jakobsson, and Christer Wiklund. "Winter Predation on Two Species of Hibernating Butterflies: Monitoring Rodent Attacks with Infrared Cameras." *Animal Behaviour* 81 (2011): 529–534.

Olofsson, Martin, Sven Jakobsson, and Sven Wiklund. "Auditory Defence in the Peacock Butterfly (*Inachis io*) against Mice (*Apodemus flavicollis* and *A. sylvaticus*)." *Behavioral Ecology and Sociobiology* 66, no. 2 (2012): 209–215.

Olofsson, Martin, Hannie Løvlie, Jessika Tibblin, Sven Jakobsson, and Christer Wiklund. "Eyespot Display in the Peacock Butterfly Triggers Antipredator Behaviors in Naïve Adult Fowl." *Behavioral Ecology* 24, no. 1 (2012): 305–310.

Page, Rachel A., and Ximena E. Bernal. "Túngara Frogs." *Current Biology* 16, no. 23 (2006): R979–R980.

Purdic, Kathleen L., and Jeffrey C. Oliver. "Once a Batesian Mimic, Not Always a Batesian Mimic: Mimic Reverts Back to Ancestral Phenotype when the Model Is Absent." *Proceedings of the Royal Society B: Biological Sciences* 285 (2008): 1125–1132.

Rodríguez-Robles, Javier A., and Manuel Leal. "Effects of Prey Type on the Feeding Behavior of *Alsophis portoricensis* (Serpentes: Colubridae)." *Journal of Herpetology* 27, no. 2 (1993): 163–168.

Rundus, Aaron S., Donald Owings, Sanjay S. Joshi, Erin Chinn, and Nicholas Giannini. "Ground Squirrels Use an Infrared Signal to Deter Rattlesnake Predation." *Proceedings of the National Academy of Sciences* 104, no. 36 (2007): 14372–14376.

Templeton, Christopher N., Erick Greene, and Kate Davis. "Allometry of Alarm Calls: Black-Capped Chickadees Encode Information about Predator Size." *Science* 308 (2005): 1934–1937.

Vallin, Adrain, Sven Jakobsson, Johann Lind, and Christer Wiklund. "Prey Survival by Predator Intimidation: An Experimental Study of Peacock Butterfly Defence against Blue Tits." *Proceedings of the Royal Society B: Biological Sciences* 272 (2005): 1203–1207.

Wignall, Anne E., and Phillip W. Taylor. "Assassin Bug Uses Aggressive Mimicry to Lure Spider Prey." *Proceedings of the Royal Society B: Biological Sciences* 278, no. 1710 (2011): 1427–1433.

For my boys
S. B.

For the father I never knew, who was killed in WWII
B. K.

Text copyright © 2019 by Susannah Buhrman-Deever
Illustrations copyright © 2019 by Bert Kitchen

First edition 2019

Library of Congress Catalog Card Number pending
ISBN 978-0-7636-9533-0

19 20 21 22 23 24 CCP 10 9 8 7 6 5 4 3 2 1

Printed in Shenzhen, Guangdong, China

This book was typeset in Dante MT.
The illustrations were done in watercolor and gouache.

Candlewick Studio
an imprint of Candlewick Press
99 Dover Street
Somerville, Massachusetts 02144

visit us at www.candlewickstudio.com